FACE CUT OUT FOR LOCKET

FACE CUT OUT FOR LOCKET

Jenn Blair

BRICK ROAD
POETRY PRESS

Brick Road Poetry Press
www.brickroadpoetrypress.com

For David, who has my number, but keeps on calling it anyway

Cover art: Detail from "The Gold Locket," Frederick Carl Frieseke, c. 1919

Author photo: © 2022 Katie Campbell

Library of Congress Control Number: 2021934389
ISBN: 978-1-950739-06-6

Published by Brick Road Poetry Press
314 Lee Road 553
Phenix City, AL 36867
www.brickroadpoetrypress.com

Brick Road logo by Dwight New

Table of Contents

I.

Consider...3

Cruel..4

Damascus Road..5

After the Prodigal Returned...6

Vow..7

Coffle...8

Same Old...13

Last Chore...15

Late Knowledge...16

The Christening Cup..17

Hellbender..19

A Government Man Recollects..20

Ezra, Esther, Nehemiah, Job...21

The Thirsty Stream...24

Word Came...26

Removal...28

E. Mullins' Last Confession...29

The War Ended...30

Until You Die...31

Blood Mountain...32

Papers..34

The Truth...36

Desperately Involved..37

Oxblood...39

Epitaph For a Stubborn Folk...41

Premonition..42

II.

The Ballad of Jesse Garon..45

Waterfall..47

Mayday...49

Exchange..51

The Birth..52

Ritual...53

Gold Medal..54

Our Men...55

Origins...56

Bury Me Shallow...58

Off-Season...60

Aunt Rita's Father Gets Bad News.......................................61

Terminus..62
Parade..64
Side-Lined..67
The Glory of the Morning..68
The Shedding Apostle...69
The Painter My Mother-in-Law Suggested............................71
Senior Prom, Bristol, TN..72
A New Map..74
Advancing..76
Playground...78
After the Play in a Small Town...79
Face Cut Out For Locket...80
The Flood...81
Scarcity & Want...82
Washing Instructions...83
The Sinner's Humble Request..84
Winnowing...85
Wager Last...87

Acknowledgments...89
About the Author..90

I.

this landscape hurts
as it shows me everything is real, everything
equal to its own weight
to touch it touches off the pain inside…
  —Margaret Randall, "So Many Rooms Has a House but One Roof"

Consider

the earth clinging
to the roots of wild
onions pulled from
the garden each spring
—holding fast to thin
white filament, heedless
the whole enterprise
is failing; resolute,
even when shaken—
refugees quietly
settling the shallow
lines of your palm,
still hopeful for asylum
in the murderous country.

Cruel

Starved stick bone
cows gobbling up
fat calves, skeleton
corn spitting plump
kernels from rotten
mouths, purple hills'
pinched faces turned
the very same shade
as mother Mary's
that afternoon her
firstborn son talked
back to her in front
of a crowd—wilted
and shamed and what
was it for—sleep
shorn nights, sore
engorged breasts
wracked with rivers
of stone, tender
shards of shared
mornings, evenings
and afternoons swiftly
ground away in *woman,*
what does that concern me?

Damascus Road

Youth-folly.
When I had the cream skin
I was a sinner.
Cavorting in each square
lifting my shapely leg
to piss in the fountains of God.
Then blight snapped
my proud princess neck,
maggots squirming around
my knocked down knees
as I gagged and praised
Holy! Holy! Holy!
My only remaining Suitor
unseen and taciturn.

After the Prodigal Returned

he kept at his big-chest strutting
around, chuckling at those of us
whose hands had stuck to the plow,
plodding animals with no imagination
but to obey. His first Sunday back
in the pew his eyes shone with rank
pride—gazing beyond slot-and-tab
tombstones to something half-coiled,
wanton—basking in butter slathered
sun. The next day his grateful family
invited us all to the fatted calf feast—
a hog yanked from the woods, its
throat promptly slit on behalf of one
who almost missed the meal prayer
on account of having gone behind
the smokehouse to regale some young
impressionables with tales of his most
recent exploits. Handed my portion
I nodded my thanks then sat down
on a nearby stump quietly chewing,
ruing the golden autumn afternoons
the charred flesh on my plate might
have spent snuffling yet for chestnut
and acorn scattered across the forest
floor, its dripping snout quivering,
full of honest enjoyment.

Vow

Near the end, she babbled, wanting
things. Whenever we held up a spoon
of chicken broth to her pale worm lips
she'd push it away—punishing herself
as my mother rushed to the other room
to weep for this shriveled up creature
who once tore both her hands plucking
her baby the juiciest blackberry God ever
strung inside a thick crown of thorn.
The night father took down his fiddle
and began to play *Ora Lee* she screeched
so loud the wood flew away from his chin
and almost broke—startled varnished bird.
Given all the trouble she was causing,
I wished she would—just once—bolt up
crying *I see bright living souls nailed into coffins*
of flesh, buried angels swimming deep in the grain.
To speak of the winter fox or blood moon
creeping nearer our door. But she just lay
on her soured pillow silent, spider spittle
crusting one more circle round her mouth
as I tore off my apron and ran outside—
admonishing coal skinks sunning themselves
on flat rocks—Sal's left in the grass again
corn husk doll. *Don't take the fruit. Don't die.*

Coffle

*The Slave Trail of Tears is the great missing migration—a thousand-mile-long river of
people, all of them black, reaching from Virginia to Louisiana. During the 50 years before
the Civil War, about a million enslaved people [were forced] from the Upper South—
Virginia, Maryland, Kentucky—to the Deep South—Louisiana, Mississippi, Alabama.*
   —Edward Ball (*Smithsonian*)

A man with a white
hat and coat the color
of those mushrooms
you never eat, loud
talking, ruled the show.
Mr. big stripey britches
sat way up on a horse
holding a gun like a baby
he sometimes put down
to take an onion out
of the mushroom coat
and grab a quick bite
and what came after
was two by two by two
by two of men glued
together with a long
silver chain followed
by women with rope
tied round their scabbed
wrists and the sound
of hundreds singing,
a short man with a banjo
hopping around playing
the same dumb tune
and when he was done
he'd just start it again,
bobbing his fat neck
while his skinny friend
threw his little pale

8

arms out and out
wider and wider
so the voices wouldn't
stop and the dusty feet
would stay in step
with other dusty feet
"As I went up the new-cut road/
I spied a possum and a toad"
you never seen so
many bodies filing
by, an army of stinking,
sweating bug-bit open
-sored legs marching
over the land followed
by a parade of creaking
wood wagons stuffed
with old and maybe
sick folks because
there was coughing
and some groaning
and there were kids
walking too, girls
who wouldn't look
over at me and a boy
my age or a year older
biting his lip til it bled
and there were men
loudly cracking whips
and doing a lot of yelling:
'don't drag behind—
only seven more miles
for the day,' men saying
whoever sang loudest,
man, woman, or child
with the biggest pipes

would get themselves
a treat—a wide chunk
of fresh green granny
apple *Mr. Emerson will judge*
and since nothing much
ever really happens here
I started walking behind
though a man with one
bent ear that looked
chewed by a dog yelled,
"Scat, girl" but I didn't
listen and kept following
til the two by two by two
came to the dock of the
River New, that great
gushing swerve of water
daddy sometimes fishes
if he gets a day off,
and they had the string
of raggedy men wade
right in as if they were
supposed to be Moses
parting the river
but the river didn't
part, cold water
up to their waists
chests and necks
and still they sang,
higher and louder
no Noah's ark
just the flood
and them pairs
yelling out words
about proud gals
and eating mush

as the mushroom
coat man still sat
up there on his horse
smoking a cloud,
yelling "easy, easy
boys, if one slips
the rest will follow"
and before I could
even start to think
or worry about
them all drowned
they started flinging
women and children
on flatboats, shoving
them off as the silvery
chain started dancing
again and the men
wound tight about
that silvery chain
stepped up onto
the other bank,
dripping and singing
*I wish I was back
in Old Kentuck*
singing as they went
some other place
that must have been
even farther away
from wherever it
was they came
than ever before
so I turned back
and when I sat
at the table that
night my mother's

stupid-dead eyes
said *what did you*
see made you so late
and the look I shot
back said   *nothing*
then father said—
without even caring
where have you been
and I said *nowhere*
taking a bite of beet,
chewing it to mash
and pulp as a fresh
stone crying LIAR
LIAR LIAR popped
up in the graveyard
behind the church.

Same Old

Feed me thick enough
water, gruel gussied up
with two thick pinches
or more of potato flour
and I'm scared I'll start
dreaming again about
cakes lined up on lace
paper doilies, regal ones
tall as hats, sugar dust
specking the warm, hot
air—pink and blue iced
roses with yellow leaves
not yellow 'cause they're
sick—just a noble fine
color curling all around.
So much fuel in my gullet
I begin to believe I'll be
welcomed in and offered
any toothsome I want—
told to keep on eating
til a big hole gobbles up
the famished sky, a silver
fork with a soft ribbon
thrown into my blistered
hand. In that poisonous
glittering dream, everyone
real or not real I've ever
loved, adored, or wanted
to talk to for just a minute
(please) is there but I'm not
begging, I'm the honored
guest, the only interesting
thing, no one glancing

past my raisin burned face
to see who's strolling in next.

Last Chore

Leave abstraction (cold, unfathomable
as Christ's dead brow) for the pail's
worn wood handle—erstwhile pining
for curry comb bristles still panting
with flecks of skin and glistening hair.
No more 'where oh where is God's
stoutest truth' pointing towards
the stars then towards your scrawny
caved in chest useless poet mooning!

Last night we lost a calf to that.

The world you can't ever seem
to find without blacking your
eye—bruising your shin is here—
its membranes and fluids smeared
in my boots' rusted eyelets.

Before you step in this house again,
wade out to the end of these sun
scorched rows and whistle sharp—
retie your skittish mind to its
stern tether of sinew and shank—
the subtle, more dependable wiles
of porch-light, leaf-litter, bone rot.

Late Knowledge

The sluggish ridge and its correspondingly
drab shingle of low slung sky, one promise
made to a man whose reflection was dull
as my own, twin lice tucked away in the woods
to fester, wane, decompose under smoldering
cinnamon fern til I almost cursed our stale
breath and stove-smoke hair, all the sloughed
off bodies our lackluster bed gradually accrued,
resenting their endless needs and wants while
trudging the long path harnessed hairpin
tight to the day's demands, an ass too stupid
to notice the light was already changing
until a thin strand of geese steadily laboring
overhead finally allowed me to see this place
as a traveler coming in from far away must
view it—wideness flaring in the narrow acre—
the surrounding hills remaining themselves
even as they became something else entire,
barns, hayfield, and pond swiftly transfiguring,
everyone else too intent on their darning, raking,
hoeing, mending—too busy enjoying dusk's
allotted few minutes of precious casual chatter
to hear two small sorry knots of fist pounding
against the pane, begging to be let in.

The Christening Cup

He awoke to a bitter in the saliva,
itching between neck and collar
he had not counted. Sitting up,
he slowly blinked his eyes awake
to a ring of drying sedge strung
around his weary body. Barking
for attention, no one answered.
Out in the front parlor, the Bible
box was empty save for the seeds
already set aside for next year's
crops, the heavy book therein
splayed out on its Battenberg
doily—a few strands of Timothy
hay marking Daniel chapter four—
the wild tale of a self-righteous
King driven out of the castle
of his once impenetrable mind
til his lips foamed green grass,
head bent like dumb cattle.
Enraged, he went and picked
up a skillet teeming with clover
off the kitchen stove and hurled
it to the floor, breaking the plates
and dishes she must have filled
til he arrived at the last item
and sank down, astonished.
Hadn't she thrown every dark
curl away, buried the rabbit
spoon the neighbor carved,
burned the blue quilt she'd
stayed up late every night
those last months stitching—
all the come before names strung
bright in the tree, sudden ash.

When he found the courage to lift
it to his lips, it began to tremble,
a buzzing rim of wasp, a living rebuke.

Hellbender

she shucked her eyes.
left her tongue. took it off,
set it on a flat granite rock
for ravens to peck/salamanders
to roost as she walked further
and further into the woods,
hands cupped to catch
whatever small speckles
of light managed to filter
all the way down through
the branches, sifted minnows
darting across her thirsty palms.

A Government Man Recollects

A few of those hardest to reach places were almost smothered in Hackberry and Trumpet Creeper—frail toeholds barely discernible from rock and the hillside itself—the women inside wearing bludgeoned faces which might have been considered delicate once, back before the limestone's drip, drip, drip all but eroded their brows, chins and mouths—women with exasperated veins bulging up along the uneven ridges of mosquito bit hands.

When we'd ask to speak to their men, they'd hesitate then leave for what seemed like an hour before returning—their dull bird dung eyes glancing to the other side of the soot filled room trying to ascertain what width of crust they could offer while their husbands' obdurate necks puffed with pride and outrage—to have to give something more still—so that we always were taught to quickly reply *No thanks, ma'am* if they ever offered a slab of apple stack-cake or modest slice of molasses bread, to speak our sober bit of progress then ride away at a quick gallop, deaf to any shrieks or cries rising up behind slammed shut doors.

Ezra, Esther, Nehemiah, Job

He should have despised the face
which re-appeared in the well—
soundly condemned the changeling
who'd dared fasten my mother's
fine mouth to her own greedy lips
to utter her first cry, but, instead,
how quickly she came to rule!
Taunts all—how she held her
hands in the exact same fashion
and tilted her head just so, her
instep light and fleet and possessed
of a strange alchemy which held
my father transfixed. Never once
did he look at me—wearing his
close-set eyes and harsh-angled
chin in that same fashion for he
had no use for himself and thus
dismissed me—made me share
in his contempt. I meekly endured
and accepted til the April morning
the bracelet first appeared on her
wrist, a gold chain dripping a seed
-pearl turtle, the fabled prize of my
mother's youth, bequeathed to her
on the day she'd finally (after much
heartbreak and needless inversion)
correctly recited all sixty-six books
of the Bible in the proper order.

Seeing it on her arm, I ran outside
and wept. What should have been
the firstborn's—stolen. But the day
I crept into her room to take it off
her dresser, a shadow fell over

21

the sun which never left even as we
packed our things and rode away
for the last time from that cruel slip
of earth where I learned I was nobody.

Only now that my eyes have grown
old and weak am I finally starting
to see how some souls can't ever
manage to rise up out of grief.
Perhaps my father needed to value
my sister most, on account of her
taking what he most valued—
and she—she was never my
enemy—just another lonely child
who'd entered sad circumstances
unknowing. So time had softened
my resolve but not my shame
the afternoon a tear rolled down
her cheek as she sat on the couch
in my den recalling how careless
she must have been to lose it—
the jewelry it surely took our
mother so many hours to earn.
I should have confessed right
then, but I said nothing save for
a silent, murderous hand on hers.

As deaconesses from *Living Waters*
begin building babel high towers
of ham and egg salad sandwiches
on the new kitchen counter she'll
never have the chance to enjoy,
I excuse myself and—in the few
moments I have alone with her—
lean over the casket and kiss her
forehead—pouring my confession

into her and my mother's sweet
ear—shaking fingers barely able
to un-hook, hook the clasp.

Later, there at the graveside,
my three children glance
at each other, concerned,
so ebullient is my countenance.
How to even begin to tell
them of it?! The sudden
sharp dazzle, stones of light
dropping straight down
through your ribs and never
hitting, the terror and relief
to glimpse all hates and loves
hurdling to naught.

The Thirsty Stream

When father's lectures grew
briefer we beamed and straightened
believing ourselves growing in grace
and stature, not noticing at first
his skin souring to candle tallow,
eyes darting farther back into their
sockets as he walked unsteadily
across fields he'd once plowed.

Right as we closed the coffin
a cloud about the size of an
infant's cheek carved itself out
of the sky, a smudge quickly
darkening. The first drop of rain
in months. All the mourners
gathered worked hard to hide
their joy, a few gracious mumbles
before hurrying home to tremble.
Mother, always sensible, suddenly
believed him down in hell,
the minister's unique assurances
failing to calm her writhing mind.

What he had done she did not say
but every day thereafter she stopped
to drink a full glass of water the same
space of time he fell, to quench him,
bone of her bone writhing in flame.

After she stopped swallowing, her
children and grandchildren took turns
dabbing her lips with small chips of ice.
One afternoon a distracted daughter,
rushing through the ministrations

more swiftly than usual, elicited
the four final words: *give him some more.*

Word Came

There would be
no other season.

We kept on sweeping
floors and scouring
out greasy meatloaf
pans, pausing only
to send condolence
cards with clumps
of white lily—crowns
of brown cat-tail
ringing a placid pond
(*may golden memories bring*
peace at this difficult time).
Afternoons, we still
went out to the garden,
plucking startled fat
beetles off chewed
to lace okra leaves,
drowning them in
jars of dish soap
while tentatively
revising our mothers'
and grandmothers'
battered, lost recipe
cards on our tongues,
turning our yellowed,
oleo stained tongues
to livid brains trying
to recall: half or three
-fourths a teaspoon
of vanilla? A little more

flour or cornstarch
to thicken the broth.
If desired. Desire.

> *were we once girls.*

Removal

As my daughter turns
from me, weary with
sickness, I travel back
til I'm the one burning
on the couch beneath
a pile of soft blankets,
too young to understand
the sudden ravages of illness.

I see a sad confused face
staring up at the ceiling,
dimly curious where its
other self has gone—
doubtful if the confident
clatter of patent leather
shoes on sandstone steps
will ever return or trees rush
by again, each line of leaf
a green lit match struck
against the still defiant
chin of the lowering sun.

Eventually my mother
appears in the background
scrubbing the kitchen table
and as I watch her work,
dipping then re-dipping
her cloth in a bucket of water
before wringing it dry again,
I wonder, for the first time,
what she's thinking, crying
out—terrified—I have no
place in her secret life.

E. Mullins' Last Confession

I despaired when I first understood
the greased, expected word rolling
off my tongue was a lie stinking up
my breast. Do you think that makes
me a traitor? Wanting to get along.
Not having anyone worry or pray
for my lost soul. Everyone else's
head bowed neatly after the sermon
but what discord rattled around inside?
Or was I the sole unquiet. Never
brave enough to ask, I never knew.
How many hours did I spend
staring at that faded and tack laden
map of Paul's three missionary
journeys in the Sunday school
room right beside the kitchen?
staring at all those blue and orange
tangles of arrow thinking *shit*.
Judge me how you will, but if faith
is a gift, who is the Giver and how
does He portion it out? What if He
wanted to see me wrestle a scrap
(for testing or sport I can't say).
I may have mumble-mouthed
the hymns, relieved to arrive
at the last verse and sit again,
but I've been out in my rows
at dusk, the sun sunk low and red
in such a way anybody would tremble,
bow the knee. Anybody would say
sorry would say *thank you*—words I
cradle in my arms now one last time,
my widow's mite, my spindle-lamb,
shivering and present on the altar.

The War Ended

nineteen days before
he was scheduled
to fly his plane over.
Whenever an insect
buzzes through
the rooms of his house,
we all yell and point
as he runs to the kitchen
to grab the pink plastic
swatter his wife keeps
atop the photograph
slicked refrigerator.

Afterwards, he hums,
studiously wiping off
an errant leg and eye
with a paper towel
before taking out
a permanent marker
to make another 'X',
all the careful, precise
cross-hatches slowly,
steadily adding up.

Until You Die

you live
and this
has always mystified me.

Until it's your number,
you have one.
And you keep baking bread
and being hopeful,
scattering crumbs of old
dreams out of your pockets.
For the birds.

And you keep straining in the mirror,
looking for beauty,
but after that—and first and foremost—
the Answer.

How dark the glass; how bright these mornings.

Blood Mountain

Those first dawns and evenings
someone else washed and carried
my body, a peculiar roughness
and grace in their movements,
as if they were privy to my pain
but also must make me understand
that the day's demands continued.
So I learned to be still. In fits.
As a boy I tore over the hills,
ripping branches from trees
then pressing fresh victims
to murder, toppling over rocks
where white grub-worms cowered,
thrashing Adder's Tongue ferns,
tearing away the jagged silk swaths
black and yellow garden spiders
wove in the dense abdomens
of their intricate web, delighting
(as only a child can) in failure.
The first time a hand smacked
my jaw, I sunk to the ground,
forced to, for the first time,
consider my heart's contents
of bitterness, lust, and shame.
Then one night, the fool's dream.
That I could take some scraps
of word and shreds of thought
and feeling, cobbling them
together with nails and pins
into a startling new arrangement,
but whether that was to make
men and women glad they had
lived upon the earth or merely
to fashion a name for myself

I hardly dared to look too far
into, my hot brain spinning
wide in a pent up valley
with sides so steep I barely
noticed the light already going.
Ringing round every honest
object. Asking it to speak.

Papers

Byron Herbert Reece (1917-1958)

Whatever was going to happen next must have
been temporarily pushed aside to concentrate
on the missing comma/comma splice/awkward
run-on sentence spilling over line after line/
the overeager student's usual too much fullness
/any attempted meaning jumbled in oceans
of intensifiers while the sullen, distracted boy
who sat in the back row adjusting his tan watch
band for the better part of the hour would do
well to elucidate: "Interesting. Try to develop
this point a little further." One of three papers
he stapled together belonged to the perfectionist
who, almost in tears after class, apologized.
Adding an introductory colon to a dropped
quote, he reminded himself again not to skew
too low or high, overindulge in wrath or forgiveness,
even if the number alone decided if its eventual
recipient felt more sorrow or scorn when the news
broke. The brilliant girl who wore ill-fitting blouses
the color of egg yoke and a perpetual scowl:
And why should the dead judge me? He usually didn't
bother to correct it—the familiar misspelling
of his name, but this time, decided to strike a line
through the unnecessary "s," the new blue "c"
floating above it one last small nod to himself.
He hardly noticed them anymore—coffee-rings,
apple-flecks, salt-smears, water droplets harvested
from an exuberant sneeze. But for all they gave
him he had not asked, it wouldn't be fair to mar
their tentative thoughts, well phrased or no,
with merciless red marks. Stacking the papers
up in a neat pile, he placed them in his top desk

drawer, shutting it all the way, to keep them safe,
then stood, walking over to the wooden shelf
holding the campus apartment's record player,
scratched needle already positioned right before
that note Mozart rips open the slumbering air.

The Truth

When the chipped
Bakelite blathered
about love, eternal,
fair and fine, I was
never convinced.

Kept in the back,
I peeled potatoes
and if a bit of rough
skin stuck on mine
I did not flick it off
until I was done
and to me
that was tenderness.

Desperately Involved

with themselves they send him to the Matriarch with one wire
thick white hair sprouting out the mole on her cheek—a frill-
less woman whose freezer is crammed full of bags of haricot
beans and Silver Queen corn, pale teeth beyond the numbering.
That first night there she hands him a toothbrush and water
cup, then has him fold his clothes, place them on the chair
and kneel: "Jesus is always on the cross, and *He can hear you*."

He likes the frayed book spines locked in the glass cabinet.
The truck with a hornet's nest inside its open glove box.
The back closet smelling of camphor and a hundred summers.

Hoeing, raking, weeding, dusting, washing—she only allows
the pair one pause—a three pm radio program which invites
callers to share prayer requests and miracles, the wine-wrecked
liver which has just un-pickled itself inside a penitent sinner
down in Fitzgerald: "Even as I lay there weeping and knowing
my life was just all over, there came a stillness and then I felt
it sudden turn, leprosy swiftly succumbing to snow and gold."
While she closes her eyes (to better imagine its Resurrection),
he unhooks the latch and runs past blackbirds stealing pebbles
from the dog's pie plate, disappearing into the tall thin pines
whose shadows mow the alfalfa field's edge each afternoon.

Lying there, he falls asleep and dreams of visitors: a tall gaunt
man in a seersucker coat who passes by, but not before he takes
off his hat and stoops down beside him whispering, "I have seen
clear through my brown cankered eye to kingdoms not yet born."
Then there's the girl with the sturdy legs and a purple welt on her
arm, the one who always sits beside him making clover chains.
The girl who never speaks, until the day she bolts up, brushing
grass and gnats off her skirts. She hears voices—encouraging ones
—and kind—who've told her there's a place way back inside the Live
Oak and Cypress for children no one wants and that the only map

which could guide them there has been sewn inside someone's left palm. As he begins to uncurl his shaking fingers   MATTHEW WHERE ARE YOU   GET BACK HERE RIGHT THIS INSTANT

Oxblood

The boy from Pound is back
in the corner by the Kalmia
by the ditch, but someone
loved him—surely—his
lichen-bit grave tenderly
embedded with Cat's Eyes,
Sulphides, Chinas, and fire
-flecked Onionskins—though
one socket's prize must have
been long ago plucked out
by the bastard hands of wind,
time, rain. I've lost count
of them by by now—how
many evenings I've stooped
down to rip away the Bitter-
cress and Creeper trying
to wrap green greedy arms
round his crumbling stone.
If he wasn't taken so quick,
I like to think he would have
gone on to do great things
and perhaps even made
a woman glad—brushing
her tangled hair while talking
words soft and agreeable as lard.

One morning the boy will
return riding a pale horse,
righteousness burning out
of the bit and bridle of both
his brown eyes while the storm
clouds piled up over the far
hill begin to roil—trees shaking
as the impure swiftly scatter,

the glittering world we nearly
choked each other to obtain
revealed to be nothing more
than an old vile seedpod
belching forth dank spores
into the appalled ash-coated sky.

Epitaph For a Stubborn Folk

We made love
in small rooms,
our ardor and anger
spine fused twins
with outward turned
faces lashed together
inside the withered
husk of a great blindness.
We lived hundreds
of miles inland—
continually distracted
by thoughts of sea,
our eyes sometimes
brimming full of its
salt as field after field
of stunted grain became
the slow building outline
of a massive, burning
ship, every errant farm's
thin, steady porch light
an eruption, interruption,
of desire. Kneel down
in the thorn and Jimson.
Touch your fingers
to our bone splayed ribs.
Too many deaths here.

Premonition

Bent over laboring,
I suddenly know.
I slowly stand
and brush the dirt
off my clothes.
Without tarrying,
without haste,
I make my way
over to the far
fence where all
I have lost stands
at the field's edge,
colt-shy, defiant.

What do I do
what do I do
but there, at day's end,
wordlessly nod.

II.

You see, aftermath is easier, opening
again the wound along its numb scar; it is the sentence
spoken the second time—truer, perhaps,
with the blunt edge of a practiced tongue.
        —Claudia Emerson "Aftermath"

The Ballad of Jesse Garon

I arrived in the frost-cold, blue lips
spilling onto stained sheets, no sharp
bleat to exalt my mother's exhausted
heart, my father, young, nervous—
weeping as his own father told him
to lift the lantern and prepare for another;
as dawn began furiously licking the edge
of the dog's empty bowl, I perched
on the ceiling of that thimble-house—
when he tumbled out she threw her
weary arms around him murmuring
(*sweet, darling boy, my sweet boy*)
as they rushed to the nearby hospital.
But I never felt any envy, only pity
for those poor, uneducated country
folk who only managed to rustle me
up a shoebox for an unmarked grave
in Priceville before giving what little else
they had to my brother. As the years
passed, I'd watch him take out his guitar,
shaking my head at another torn chord,
helping him bear it whenever he was made
fun of for his hand-sewn hick clothes.
I carried it too. The bitter pebble he took
in his mouth all the way up to Memphis,
until I commanded he spit it out in that
slow boiling mud wracked river that my
joyous shouts might animate his feet,
my un-spent dreams turn to unspooled
velvet gushing over his loosened tongue.
Yes, I did hear a woman say it once,
a particularly unimaginative woman

whose over-stuffed ankles could barely
traverse the R.V. cluttered parking lot
to the gift shop's magnets, snow-globes
and decorative spoons: *I mean, of course*
he wilted up right away, if you was up
against all that why would you even bother?
I began chuckling so loud she must have
felt an inexplicable ringing clog up her fat
ears. I didn't stoop to blame her for how
could she, dumb and priceless as she
was, understand how I began to burn
in that secret place, a furnace radiating
such intense majesty that the maggot
wadded in beside me put his nub-
webbed limbs over his still forming
face, to hide and shield it—a worm
so over-awed that I knew I must take
pity. Later, he would pray up to me
at night as he lay on his bed in the dark,
promising to buy me the most expensive
pink marble stone, a fancy obelisk writ
with roses and my full name upon it—
he would work hard at one job and then
another and another to collect enough
dollar bills for a proper Ebenezer at last
and that is how I'll always remember him,
this babe, this boy, this bloated American
lamb who always had to carry the water
to the well alone while vainly laboring
to re-create the tiniest little sliver-glimpse
of my G-damn *thank you Jesus* glorious light!

Waterfall

The guidebook waterfall.
Fulsome.
Waterfall this morning.
Scant.
Prediction for tomorrow's waterfall:
Better and steady.

Location: 500 yards west of the authentic
rustic old inn, ever hospitable, mauve napkins
spread fans, three eggs scrambled, sweat
dewed sausage links/parsley sprig. Carefully
still uncurling citrus ribbon. The full effect.

Unmediated: The waterfall that was falling
before encroachment, before hearsay began,
water falling into every space but the pupil and iris.
No children allowed (No children EVER allowed).

Waterfall. A question: Was it all you expected?
Lie: Oh yes. Now I feel like a real_____(insert
nationality here).

Honeymoon: Two lost people standing in front
of a waterfall. Holding hands: optional.

Plunder: The black and white sketch of the waterfall
which first appeared in the explorer's notes, grafted
to droplets of civilization, fish torn from the corner,
magic leached scales, a silver tray full of faces drowned.

Erasure: A woman's lips drawn tightly owing to an especially
angular piece of gravel from the waterfall trail now speeding
away with her in the train, the ground crying to go back home
versus being pent inside a fashionable laced up leather boot.

Depression: Was THAT the waterfall?

Jealousy: The tall stone wall and sign: "Private. No Visitors"

Yearning: The swath of water that must be falling right now,
at this very moment, behind the stone wall. Rare. Select. Pristine.

Memory: The postcard back still bristling:
"Lovely." "Much impressed to witness."
All heaven's fury contained in the cramped
expansive confines of the brain and eye
before being briskly catalogued and stored
between two other (though who ever knows
exactly which two other) dust covered plates.

Source: Where water (the falling) began.
Green ferns. Mossed rocks. God's Mouth
(God meaning infinite pleasure).

Mayday

Living all these years with the knowledge, I unintentionally had a small part in trying to tell the world a truth, it, as a whole did not care to hear, and the accompanying criticism makes one feel unnecessary at times.
   —Nina Paxton, Ashland, KY (July 22, 1968)

Wear thick serviceable shoes. When you arrive
at each bedside, adjust the sheets and your tone
accordingly, briskly cheerful or more subdued.
Dispense hope, but if someone asks if it's bad
and it is, don't lie—for the dead know the truth,
such as the man whose chest fell directly under
the machine which spits out steel at Armco mill.
Understand that some, at the last, bear up, while
others suddenly falter. Expect to be privy to pain.
And heaven. The oil refinery worker who lost an eye
in an explosion telling his weeping daughter who'd
just rushed in that his remaining one might collapse
under the weight of so much beauty. Some, already
stressed, buckle, the woman who broke her arm
and leg and lost her mother's prized Fox and Geese
wedding quilt that one winter the Ohio flooded
its banks staring up at the stained ceiling whispering
this isn't my life this isn't my life as if the saying might
make it so. Try to meet each of them where they are,
keep them comfortable as you can, and when the shift
is finally over, go home and prepare yourself a little
dinner. Cast off your soiled uniform and flop down
by the console, exchanging frail bodies for the luxury
of hale, nimble voices darting through the waves.
Try to relax. Close your eyes and rotate your tense
shoulder blades, but if the hospital's loud noises
and urgency come roaring back over the wire—
—someone's in distress—there's been a crash,
a person injured—jump up at once to jot down
the details. After that, do everything in your power

to try and help. Call and write carefully crafted letters
—give obliging interviews year after year, even if no
one listens. Even if they say that someone in another
time zone surely would have heard the aviator as well.
Smile. Be professional. Remain polite when they call you
Mistaken. A bit confused—gently inferring that a life
as ordinary and middle-aged as yours must have been
in such need of attention you went ahead and invented
the fantastical tale: a woman asking a woman for help.

Exchange

His brother, leg took off by a tractor accident,
bunkers up in their room scrawling supplications
in a marble-mottled 99 cent composition book every
chance he gets, pages crammed so full of wild, endless
praises and plans he doesn't even bother glancing up
when his own flesh stands in the doorway to announce
he's going fishing on Glades Rd. with the Halson twins.

He liked it better when his brother wasn't so sanded down,
a laughing impish boy brushing right up against the world
with a wide grin, shoulders swaying through it easily, loosely,
as if he were welcome, were at home. He'll die with it half
-rotted under his eye-lids, the cut of the engine—sickening
silence—their father running towards the house, arms full.

When he lost that limb, he found a new passion for his Lord
—their grandmother, voice low and factual—seemingly
satisfied with a jealous God's arithmetic. She doesn't know.
None of them do. About the other numbers he keeps.

One night he dreams Judas comes to their door, knocks,
then refuses to enter. Noose still hanging around his neck
the traitor politely stands out on their porch, guilty fingers
clasped behind his maggot wracked spine: was this house
hold ever informed that eleven months, five days, three
hours and six minutes ago, their youngest son kept a '83
and '78 quarter out of the purple-mouthed offering plate?
As his mother begins to wail, his father's face darkens,
while his brother only slowly—mysteriously—smiles.

The Birth

The red wet
smear slipped out
then down
onto the straw—
a bubbling
afterthought
the flies flew near
before changing
courses.
Did you see it,
mother asked
as we drove away
from the farm,
her eye on the curve
not my knees clasped
close together.

Ritual

She will pretty herself for the boy
whose acoustic guitar pants for holiness,
the one who looks to no girl in the pew
but up past the angels with pinched
together eyes and unconvincing hands
donated by the rich woman who flew
to stain-glass classes after her husband's
unforgiving second stroke. She bought
the white and peach box at the grocery,
relieved by its promise to lighten the dark
hair she detests, the cover which sends
her to class in long sleeves and keeps her
sweltering at summer camp. Safely home,
she sits on the bathtub's edge and mixes
the crème with the powder, uses the little
pale plastic shovel to cake her disgrace,
trying not to breathe in the sharp fumes.
We're Scottish, we needed to keep warm
in those cold high hills—her father's only
offering the one time she dared to ask
it aloud—what was wrong with her.
When she can no longer stand the burning,
she washes the mixture off, carefully
examining each stipple of scorched skin.
If the boy sings tonight in his tasteful
worn denim, let the praise go straight
to God but if his ice blue eye happens
to snag on the swaying arms, may hers
be found to be the smoothest in the sea,
all their former unruliness golden-ed,
thinned, and chastened. Let him follow
them far enough along to find them
attached to a soul hungry as his own.

Gold Medal

Before those elaborately eye-lashed dolls
with wads of intricate internal machinery
arrived, all the boys and girls taking Home
Economics at my town's high school
were made to care for babies made of flour.
For a full two and a half weeks they'd tote
around ten pound sacks to class, soccer,
cheerleading, and the library before heading
to the bus or their parents' old automobiles.
In the end, perhaps the heft *was* the lesson,
the inconvenience of shifting bulky corners
and giving costly attention to something that
didn't utter one peep of thanks—while all
the while fearing springing a leak and leaving
a guilty trail of white soot down the sweat
infested hallway after gym, history or math.
Ultimately, it was a not-so-subtle form of birth
control—a mandatory assignment for blushing
teenagers to groan and laugh at, one my own
mother might have recalled a few years later
as she stood in her minuscule kitchen shifting
me awkwardly on her hip, seized with a sudden
strange desire to bake a warm loaf of bread.

Our Men

come into the world a little too hot to trot
spun way up, tossing down the milk bottle,
fists curled in the crib, my brother waking
so sweaty they had to cut the plastic feet
out of his zip-up pajamas, his damp toes
leaving a set of animal tracks down the hall,
my father honking his horn at anyone going
too fast or slow on the road or failing to flick
on their turn light, my mother begging him
to hold back the middle finger at that one
especially treacherous curve where people
going too fast cross the middle line, *these days*
any nut can walk right out of the shop with a gun!
my grandfather all but quietly bawling when
the pine strand at the edge of the south pasture
browned and spindled, *his praying place*, grandma
informed us wiping her hands on faded apron
ducks, *the only place he ever felt like God liked him.*

It's as if none of them ever got the letter about
it being a difficult land, the faucet's drip-drip-drip
steadily taking away what small fortunes we may
have hoarded in fatter times, my Uncle crawling
into the casket as the last hymn played as a mix
of elders and deacons pried him loose and sat him
back in the pew, sparse eyed, gulping down glass
after glass of dry air as the piano triumphantly
tinkled towards some far off, rumored victory.

Origins

Officer, I can explain. It all began
with a cat skull she found in our
alfalfa field, one pearly-dull tooth
shining in the sun she held aloft
like Charlemagne's Chalice or cup
of eternal salvation. Those arched
eye-sockets split her life in twain.
Afterwards, she was out by the side
of the road at all hours, always
intent on bringing something back.
Shed valise of snake, cicada husk,
beetle prongs, armadillo back, three
paws she cut off of some road kill
and plopped in a mayonnaise jar;
(what animal exactly I don't recall).
That's why this house doesn't sort
memories by Christ pinned to cross
but moth-wing on cotton batting,
owl excrement in brown un-salted
butter tubs waiting to be tweezed
for treasure—dead lizard excavations,
patient probings for recalcitrant hearts.
She wasn't ever that *off*. Just curious.
She would have taken up Van Gogh's
ear (if VG didn't mind and really was
done with it), rushed it home to her
room and sat on her bed face a-flush
with good fortune before beginning
to coo lovely nothings to that artist's
famously perturbed soul on the slight
chance some invisible trembling string
might still attach the two, my sweet
St. Francis girl softly singing—ear
a fast-calming down bird so happy

to be caught in the nest of her
delicate hands, fingers tapered
thin as her poor, deceased father's.

Bury Me Shallow

for the dead shall rise to meet the Lord
in the air and I shall not wait.
Some years ago, when I needed
more money, I promised the guilty
daughter four states away I would
routinely visit the partitioned room
full of bric-a-brac bingo figurines,
dimple-cheeked children holding
polka dot umbrellas, and animals
weighed down by overwrought
eyes, and so I did, ignoring odors
from low sodium soups and failing
bowels while shouting out verses
from the petunia soaked devotional
the minister had left—listening
to unmemorable memories of hogs
getting loose in the yard again—
the morning her philanderer Uncle
rode by in a new Ford with a new
wife and a new hat, furiously honking.
Though the doctors kept feathering
their tones, her sallow face knew.
By then, the inattentive daughter
had passed away so I bent low beside
her bed, taking up her gnarled hand
(more root and burn than shape)
as she asked it again: *Bury me shallow.*
Hearing her request, my throat grew
raw for the God she adored had not
kept my sister or I safe night after night
over so many years, but this woman
was a wild bloom in my life, so I
carefully snipped gold jingle bells
off red Dollar Tree stockings, sewing

them onto the softest wool slippers
I found at Sears, my neat even stitches
the one prayer I'd concede: that she
would fly up quick as she wished
and that He in whom she so delighted
would hear her feet coming then rush
to fall prostrate before her, swiftly
handing her back all her praise.

Off-Season

Light in the fields, flat,
each grazing cow, sad,
commonplace. Houses
shingled scabs clinging
to the earth's tired side.
Dull river stone shorn
of its summer flesh,
laughing scars slowly
drifting along on pink
/orange/yellow tubes.

The *Mountain Glimpse
Motel* sitting behind
an empty diving board
rusting a few feet above
a kidney shaped patch
of henbit, carpetweed
and burclover, the few
cars parked in its lot
covered in tan shroud.

*Amish butter! Wicker!
Last gas for twenty-two miles!*
But it was an untested
love, love over-stuffed
with fudge and geode.

Bell collared goats
on a roof absented
for winter, masticating
now in shameful private,
shrill red roadside arrow
on warped, cracked board
pointing to naught.

Aunt Rita's Father Gets Bad News

At the doctor's office he only nodded,
picked up his coat, and left. One month
later, they found his truck on the reservation.
His relatives searched for awhile, then went
out to his garage and found enough for two
yard sales. End tables. Lamps. A dusty line of
stuffed quail traveling along a lacquered log.
Myriads of caps for an army of heads, coffee
mugs, fans, car batteries, even a strange belt-
contraption rumored to vibrate off a belly.
Still in perfect working order, an impressed niece
commented as his giggling grandchildren
waited to take their turn inside the machine,
smart modern children, shaking, laughing—
perfectly dispossessed of the puerile belief
they would ever walk away thinned down.

Terminus

I.

Dog barking, barking, barking
wanting something, something still.
She never once told him about it.
The money continually siphoned
off to her no good younger brother
for his cigarettes and BBQ extra
ridges potato chips. His money.
His. Not hers. The few cents he
scraped away by putting up
with rude customers and that
yammering asshole son of his
boss who didn't even know
how to put in a muffler right.
The arthritis in his hands
didn't stop him from wielding
the baseball bat to great effect.
Slowly driving back home later
that night, the sheriff recalled
how the two of them had played
together a few autumn afternoons.
All the boys from both sides
of the creek and way up Soap
Stone Rd. laughing as they raced
in the bindweed and dandelion
infested lot behind the school.

II.

Four and a half miles after the last
pull out before the double hairpin
curve, the transplanted German
couple—tired of scooping endless

samples of chocolate pistachio
and mint with impossibly small
hot pink plastic spoons—finally
decided to sell their crumbling faux
Bavarian building—its painted on
cottage curtains permanently lilted
up by some magical unseen breeze—
then vanished to Pensacola. Six
months later, a few pitiful stacks
of thin vulcanized tires appeared
out front and then a smattering
of people began stepping from
cars still running, nervous men
and women fussing with wads
of paper bills while baleful-eyed
toddlers gummed generic sweet
potato wagon wheels in the back
seat—the town's elders grown
slack-mouthed, their hitherto
proud shoulders suddenly bent
from the way all the young folk
were trying to bypass the scenic
view for the full, vast vision,
Mary on this night and in this
county lying on her side, brain
and belly large with useless
thought, Mary swollen with pity
for herself as well as the child
whose lips even then, were blue
from cold—weaving unsteady
song to offer the dark.

Parade

Rich Allen, Lon Aycock, Claud Elder, Bob Harris, Joe Patterson, Sandy Price, Lewis Robinson, Rich Robinson, Eugene Yerby

Watkinsville, GA
June 29, 1905
December 2, 2017

It's beginning, five-six minutes past but it's beginning,
just about to begin, trembling hands re-adjusting masks
as a horse neighs, buggies rolling to a stop while children
with plastic sacks gather up and down Main Street, across
from the courthouse, in front of Oconee State Bank, pistols
and shotguns at the ready, young college couples sitting
on football dotted blankets in the grass in front of Eagle
Tavern *bang-bang-bang! Marshal! We know you're in there.*
We don't want any trouble and there won't be if you just get out
of your bed and come out. Maybe park over at Rocket Field,
we parked by the Methodist church near Attic Treasures
We don't want any trouble but if we have to come in there and dress
you like a doll then drag you out ourselves we will. Do you see us
now? On the curb right by the bleachers waving at you.
No, I'm in a red sweater, wool hat. Don't try to cross over
now though, they just did the welcome and the tractors
have already started to hum *Wake the locksmith* children
yelling and jumping up and down, waving their hands
Throw it over here, over here, upsetting their lungs for Tootsie
Rolls, smashed Laffy Taffys and stale Halloween candy,
the brave or foolish ones darting out between fire trucks,
men fumbling keys, the first middle school band marching
past as orange vests remind families to keep behind the tape
No one's sleeping here tonight, put on your shoes, boys nine bodies
rounded up and herded together, one boy whimpering
begging for stale bubblegum, flavor gone after three chews,
sudden pain at the temple *You all have got what's coming so you*
better shut up. Everyone cooing at babes placed on hay bales

by various denominations offering preschool three mornings
a week, nine men without masks, nine men walking down
the lane wearing rope around their necks, a local politician
in a grey wool coat sitting atop the back of a Corvette tossing
out Smarties *I'm innocent, I'm not who you want. You're making
a mistake. Please listen to me. Listen. Over here, over here, throw
it over here!* sanitation companies handing out stubby green
pencils with recycling logos followed by the VW contingent,
ambulances passing by without sirens, no stars but two
flickering lanterns, Clydesdales, then a newly washed truck
pulling an outhouse on a flatbed (the local historical society)
and breed-muddled dogs needing adoption gently led
on the heels of the waving chicken who adorns sacks
of nuggets and fries on Atlanta Highway. *What about
this one? He's not a . . . Don't matter! He's in jail isn't he?*
Orange sucker torn from her hands, a young girl
screams, stomping her foot, her brother gleefully
laughing until their father forces reparations, Girl
Scouts, Boy Scouts, karate groups, tap shoe serenades.
*Gentlemen, perhaps you're being a bit hasty. Why don't we
wait til the sheriff returns to help settle all this.* A young
woman in a camouflage jacket (pale, pinched face)
drops down in a canvas chair, sighing—she's eight
months pregnant—crying at everything these days.
A laundry detergent commercial with a lonely old lady.
After she begs her nephew *Shut up!* for something to eat,
he tosses her a melted peanut butter cup she gingerly
unwraps, absentmindedly licking goo from the paper.
Bring them all over here, to the fence posts. Hurry! Here comes
the one we've all been waiting for, a white bearded man
waving from the front seat of a wagon drawn by horses
in green felt antlers—and then—one last hearty *Ho-Ho-Ho*
amid and final generous spray of miniature candy canes
and cinnamon balls, *WOW! Look at all that loot! Aren't
you kids lucky? This one's still breathing. Get the doctor. Hurry!*

The street already erasing what just happened here save
for one crushed butterscotch disc, buggies rolling, horses
galloping off, masks hastily tucked into coats as cars melt
into indistinguishable traffic, rushing for a booth at *La
Parilla*, intermediate gymnastics, Simonton Bridge Road.

It's over, all finished until next year.   It's beginning, five
—six minutes past, but it's beginning   just about to begin.

Baton twirlers with lacquered scalps and bobby pinned
buns show up fifteen minutes early for one last drill.
*Step forward. Let's line up neatly like we practiced, girls. Remember
to smile big so they can see it from far away and keep those shoulders
high, don't do the droopies, everyone you know will be watching. Line
them up in a row. Tie their necks to the fence-posts. This is it, ladies!
Another knot. Tighter. No, no. Not like that. Like this. Ready? Aim.
Fire. Reload. Don't forget to listen for the first chorus on Ms. Donna's
iPhone. That'll be your cue. Fire again. Aim. Fire. Reload. Fire again.
Aim. Fire. Reload. Most importantly, don't forget to have fun! Fire again.*

Twelve small girls with rouged cheeks staring at the sky, determined,
nine frightened men bent over low, begging for the hot, steady rain
of bullets to finally dissolve, for the whirring steel to burn the face
of the sun then drop back down cool in their trembling hands.

Side-Lined

There you go,
mother cooed,
spooning two
little bacon
blobs from a
can of beans
into the garbage
as if she were
feeding a baby.

Each of my letters
to God

more terrible

brief

The Glory of the Morning

Hog-tying the fence then leaping
down to strangle another bed
of defenseless tomato plants—
blather even more pathetic kisses.
A greedy lover, it tendril-lashes
the victim it chooses, not one
but three or four times, curled
cords clutching, possessing—
desperate to possess at any price—
the kind of ill unbridled behavior
even children, bored and cross-
legged on the library's stained
alphabet rug, know to boo and hiss.

After lunch I rip away vine bare
-handed, tongue all but clucking,
then head into the garage to take
the wheelbarrow off the wall
—suddenly uneasy—sticky
green heartbreak still staining
both palms. Have I ever done
it even once. Willingly let go.
Of anything. One thing.

The Shedding Apostle

Outside, the air's amiss,
a soggy rotting sweater
or decomposing toad.
Stepping into the backyard
fearing septic trouble,
I look over at the lawn
next door and see strange
hail—a thick scattering
of mothballs on the grass,
snake repellent put out
by the righteous neighbor
who regularly sits outside
on her porch tanning her
chest and arms to leather,
and once, after an especially
memorable storm, rang
our doorbell to confess
she might be a *trespasser*
or *bad witness* because
when those strange pea
colored clouds began
to move even more swiftly,
she didn't even ask before
sneaking through our gate
to lay hands on our old
gnarled Chestnut tree—
feverishly praying it didn't
topple right onto her roof.

Sometimes I wonder,
if the Lord can't preserve
it much longer—which
direction would she or I
care for it to fall? Each

new morning it continues
to sway, we stand at our
mailboxes and smile, forked
tongues flicking politely.

The Painter My Mother-in-Law Suggested

has been dating a woman over at the college
who works in billing. She adores ballroom
dancing but doesn't mind his useless feet.
Unlike his ex, she doesn't nag him about
his motorcycle or make him green salads,
and unlike his ex, she doesn't ever finish his_____.
Last week the flabbergasting, wonderful
woman secretly mowed his whole lawn.

The painter has named the catfish in the pond
behind his house. He feeds them dog food,
just generic, but they still manage to flourish
under his benevolent hand which has sworn
off the rod. Some evenings, if he's not too
worn out, he drags a lawn chair out there
and watch the sun sink low in the pines.

This afternoon he tells me he grew up almost
next door to the notorious Civil War prison.
Many an Easter, after the dyed eggs were safely
in their wicker baskets and both ears lopped off
his Aunt's famous coconut bunny cake, he and his
cousins would roam the hills, laughing—freely
drinking from the famous spring which parched
skeletons believed the heavens, moved by their
many groans, made burble up: "I hear they won't
even let you take one tiny sip now!" he roars, brush
suspended, about to drip—then just as suddenly—
regains composure—resuming marking my door
frame with expert efficiency, admirable calmness.

Senior Prom, Bristol, TN

After hair and make-up at the mall
languishing out on Gate City highway,
she hurries the bag from Belmeade
Formal into the house—re-emerging
almost an hour later—all luminous
nervous shimmer as he jumps up
from the lawn chair where he's been
patiently waiting only to fumble—
dropping the corsage in its clear
plastic casket—clumsily parting
baby's breath with a silver pin
as they begin to laugh—her mother
(who's rushed in to help) busy
snapping endless pictures in front
of a blooming Dogwood's wide
white sleeve. As glossy brochures
depicting neat clumps of students
clutching canvas backpacks while
standing on ornate stone steps
earnestly conversing between
classes begin to clutter her desk,
he puts on another layer of flannel
while it's still dark, tractor carving
the same careful rows his scarecrow
turned father taught him the cold
April morning he lowered the blade
of his shaking hand slowly down
into the soil—fast wasting away flesh
scattering hypothetical seed from its
tremulous palm: *Just this deep. Just exactly.*

Before heading off to the new *Holiday
Inn Express* right off of 81 (Conference
Room B now a bountiful seascape

72

adorned with immense paper fish
whose scales she and three girlfriends
spent hours assiduously glittering),
they stand in the driveway for one last
shot—she reaching up to fix his bangs,
the lean firm arm encircling her waist
ending in five crescent nubs—stained
nail-beds scrubbed so vigorously with tar
-soap and water a few have begun to bleed.

A New Map

explodes on my body,
archipelagos of specks
on shoulders and breasts,
dilated blood vessels—
a topography of humility,
dense thickets of cerulean
-purple swirls on calves
and knees hopefully not
altogether unlike the spiral
and elliptical galaxies
bolting children to their
seats in awe at planetarium
shows—the thicker cords
twisting and bulging over
my ankle bones the roiling
boundaries around spaces
merely labeled—alas—or
thankfully—as parts unknown
—as if all the cartographers
decided to turn their ships
around once their bags grew
too heavy and spirits too
rueful—surmising, perhaps,
that it just wasn't what it
used to be. Glory. Fame.
Adventure. If they left right
away, there might still be
just enough time to return
and discover the same sagging
door-latch and stoop, same
slightly uneven legged chairs
around the table—a stranger
whose face still distantly matched

one they sometimes saw floating
right above their useless dreams.

Advancing

Lately, it's been peppering online threads:
fears about how much longer they'll be
able to continue. After dishing out some
hard-won advice about a Houston company's
deceptive sizing system for butternut trousers,
a recent retiree signs off from Richlands, VA—
Good luck! May you find the same share of camaraderie
my cousin and I were always so fortunate to find.
A retired electrician from Ann Arbor (chiming
in with his own suggestions), dispenses another
measure of wistful talk. His oldest granddaughter,
whose tiny skull was once comically swaddled
in gigantic hot pink headphones while she
watched papa *make the cannons go boom-boom,*
is a sophomore in college now—but a stroke
last August finally made him promise his wife
and doctor he would tell his men goodbye.
He's not the first, on either side, to desert his
post: the blistering sun seemingly hotter than
ever as it beats down on bodies lying in fields,
a raft of bad backs groaning against uneven
earth as their owners try not to squirm
(being a corpse—a young man's game)
and as for those fortunate enough to avoid
the red cartridge decreeing it their turn to fall,
knee replacement surgery slows their noble
charge up the hill even as the arthritis stealthily
creeping into fingers keeps trembling hands
from loading and reloading muskets in real time,
the excessive shaking not from fear but pain.
One by one, they're begrudgingly surrendering
to heat stroke, low blood sugar and emphysema—
the aging murmuring heart that stalls out then
must be met by a blaring, anachronistic ambulance,

medics in T-shirts, jeans, and sunglasses swiftly
overtaking the Calvary as clusters of concerned
observers in *Dick's Sporting Goods* canvas folding
chairs respectfully set down cardboard peanut
sleeves and over-priced lemonades, a mother
in purple yoga pants crushing her crying little boy
against her: *Dios, ten piedad. Please God. Por favor, ¡ayud!*

Playground

Its gloriously undulating fuzz
made the girls' eyes swoon.
As they ran back to the swings
to fetch diadems of clover,
dandelion and grass—any
possible acceptable offering
to wreathe round it—their
brother put his grey Batman
sandal on the heel of his hand
and knelt down, smashing
and smashing until every
last green drop of it had
dribbled out of its own green
mouth, then stood back up
and cheerfully shrugged,
"I don't know why I did that."

After the Play in a Small Town

The ruthlessly humbled King
in skinny jeans and a denim
jacket carrying one of those
striped tote bags the library
passed out for free last month
as he presses and re-presses
the faulty cross-walk button
on Rutherford until it jams.

The oldest, faithless daughter
wetting her pointer finger
and thumb to try and pry open
the filament of an especially
stubborn plastic sack before
squeezing an avocado, frowning.

The wise fool kneeling down
in the run amuck aisle to tuck
a grey wadded up tissue pellet
back inside each discarded shoe.

The anguished man with gouged
out eyes sitting in the duct-taped
corner booth at *El Porton*, wildly
gesticulating hands over-salting
a wire basket of stale tortilla chips.

Face Cut Out For Locket

Did she pen the note on the back
in her neat blue script to remind
a future self the mutilation hadn't
been senseless? Or were the words
mainly left there for any others
who might happen to one day
stumble across it—some small
balm that despite all the loss there
was a service in her violence, that
in this particular case, at least, her
own hands grasped the scissors.
I'm not sure why she threw herself
away then took such care to keep
herself, standing in her backyard
in a flower dotted dress, her mother's
prized Hollyhocks high as her waist,
the window behind her shoulder
opening into the garret where she
and her sisters used to put on plays
as well as dance along to music
from their father's old phonograph.
Perhaps she held onto this photograph
out of some mild fondness for familiar
scenery, but more likely it was a case
of oversight or thrift, for she had no
time for it—sentiment—this woman
I tried all my life to know. But I am
weaker than her and can't always resist—
the urge to briefly hold her body aloft
and watch light pour through.

The Flood

In the small cemetery off Cherokee
Road two women in sweat-stained
tank tops tame what's grown wild
with an old push mower and silver
clippers, busily clearing amaranth
and curled dock and yanking out
unsightly pigweed. After carefully
tending their relatives' graves, they
quickly spruce up the immediate
neighbors, but then the milk thistle
swiftly resumes, no intended slight.

It's just that they have family waiting
back at home, partners and children
impatient to salvage whatever's left
of this humid day, the work they do
here another reminder that even
the widest acts of mercy must leave
anguish at their edges, Noah and his
kin safely embracing inside the clearing
while everyone else's stone slowly
disappears beneath the grass.

Scarcity & Want

Though she begs them to stop,
her children and grandchildren
never seem to listen, buying her
another book, another scarf—
a kitchen clock with a different
brand of bird perched where
each number should be, a plastic
keyboard, terra cotta ram that
sprouts a pleasing carpet of green
fuzz once the accompanying
seed-packets have been applied
and religiously misted, a ceramic
umbrella stand with an obligatory
owl and crescent moon—a large
framed lithograph of a show she
never even watched (*Bonanza*) she
eventually deigns to hang—above
the washing machine. The worst
offender: her oldest son, who, once
retired, never leaves the cruise ship
without shopping bags in each hand.
Her last Christmas with us is the first
one she's late to the table. When she
finally appears, my brother jumps up
to pull back her chair as she slowly
sits—her rapidly shrinking body
adorned with every pearl necklace,
pair of enamel clip-on earrings, pin,
or gold bracelet she's ever received.
As my oldest cousin asks everyone
to bow their heads to pray, she stares
at the wall—a stern faced goddess
ready to depart for the underworld.

Washing Instructions

Do not I repeat put the beige sweater in the dryer.
The sleeves are already running short. Be wary
of plucking the branch from the dove's mouth.
The bird wanted to show you. That doesn't
mean he necessarily wanted you to have it.
Find forgiveness when the newest roving reporter
holds her note-pad way too high, dully reading
off her information, stumbling over her own hand
-writing as if it were a stranger's, as if nothing in
the story had absorbed her enough to remember
(the point is, the whole crop was ruined). Whisper
comfort when your dull fingers hesitate a second
too long and the gas price rolls past the perfect
OO again. One penny-two penny is not a reproach.
Underline only the crucial ("She had no notion of
death til a little chicken expired at her feet"*) without
begrudging nineteenth century fictions their endless
revelations rolling in. Bless the brown bug upturned
on its back by the kitchen garbage. How far it must
have come to impress upon you this one particular truth.

*Mary Wollstonecraft's *Mary*

The Sinner's Humble Request

Give me a symbol
I can toss in a brown lunch sack
word I can peel
poem that will stain my shirt.
Eternity's no good
if you can't wash it, mend it
it it

Winnowing

Two women grinding
grain at the mill.
Can you see them
working even now?
Look at them closely
for I tell you the truth.
One shall be taken
and one shall remain.

The terrible thrill
I felt as the pastor
solemnly surveyed
the congregation!
A precocious child
not so secretly
glancing around
the musty purple
bannered sanctuary
wondering who
among us sitting
there in our still
damp from being
recently slicked
down hair were safe.

What if I had been
brave enough back
then to turn and face
her?—this one who
keeps on laboring,
keeps on continuing
her task. This one
who, once finished,
picks up both baskets,

walking back through
flames and shouts to
feed whomever is left.

Wager Last

Perhaps if we do not love it,
it will spare us.
Perhaps if we go without names
the Summoning will cease.

Acknowledgments

"Consider" *The McNeese Review*

"The Glory of the Morning" *Kenyon Review Online*

"The Thirsty Stream" *The Chattahoochee Review*

"Waterfall" *The Berkeley Poetry Review*

"Birth" and "Epitaph for a Stubborn Folk" *Pembroke Magazine*

"Damascus" *Wraparound South*

"Aunt Rita's Father Gets Bad News" *Folia Magazine*

"Origins" *The Adirondack Review*

"Coffle" *Flock*

"Washing Instructions" *Copper Nickel*

"Edward Mullins' Last Confession," "Our Men," "Mayday,"
    Appalachian Heritage

"Hellbender," When the Prodigal Returned," "The Flood," "Papers"
    Appalachian Review

"Face Cut out for Locket" and "Ritual" *New Limestone Review*

"The Truth" *Ruminate*

"Gold Medal" *New Plains Review*

"Blood Mountain" *Broad River Review*

"The Ballad of Jesse Garon," "The War Ended" *Descant* (TCU)

About the Author

Jenn Blair is the author of three previous collections of poetry, *Malcontent* (winner of American Popular Culture's Press Americana Poetry Prize), *The Sheep Stealer* (Hyacinth Girl Press), and *All Things Are Ordered* (Finishing Line Press). Her work has been published in such journals as *Rattle*, the *Kenyon Review*, *Copper Nickel*, *Pembroke Magazine*, the *Berkley Poetry Review*, *Atticus Review*, *Southampton Review*, *Chattahoochee Review*, *Appalachian Review*, the *South Carolina Review*, *New South*, and the *Tulane Review* among others. A former recipient of Broad River Press's Ron Rash Poetry Prize and a Dorothy B. Sargent Rosenberg Poetry Award, she teaches writing at Lander University, Lee University, and the University of Georgia.

Our Mission

BRICK ROAD

POETRY PRESS

The mission of Brick Road Poetry Press is to publish and promote poetry that entertains, amuses, edifies, and surprises a wide audience of appreciative readers. We are not qualified to judge who deserves to be published, so we concentrate on publishing what we enjoy. Our preference is for poetry geared toward dramatizing the human experience in language rich with sensory image and metaphor, recognizing that poetry can be, at one and the same time, both familiar as the perspiration of daily labor and as outrageous as a carnival sideshow.

Available from Brick Road Poetry Press

BRICK ROAD

POETRY PRESS

www.brickroadpoetrypress.com

All These Hungers by Rick Mulkey

Escape Envy by Ace Boggess

My Father Should Die in Winter by Barry Marks

The Return of the Naked Man by Robert Tremmel

Available from Brick Road Poetry Press

BRICK ROAD
POETRY PRESS
www.brickroadpoetrypress.com

The Word in Edgewise by Sean M. Conrey

Household Inventory by Connie Jordan Green

Practice by Richard M. Berlin

A Meal Like That by Albert Garcia

Cracker Sonnets by Amy Wright

Things Seen by Joseph Stanton

Battle Sleep by Shannon Tate Jonas

Lauren Bacall Shares a Limousine by Susan J. Erickson

Ambushing Water by Danielle Hanson

Having and Keeping by David Watts

Assisted Living by Erin Murphy

Credo by Steve McDonald

The Deer's Bandanna by David Oates

Creation Story by Steven Owen Shields

Touring the Shadow Factory by Gary Stein

American Mythology by Raphael Kosek

Waxing the Dents by Daniel Edward Moore

Speaking Parts by Beth Ruscio

Also Available from Brick Road Poetry Press

BRICK ROAD
POETRY PRESS
www.brickroadpoetrypress.com

Dancing on the Rim by Clela Reed

Possible Crocodiles by Barry Marks

Pain Diary by Joseph D. Reich

Otherness by M. Ayodele Heath

Drunken Robins by David Oates

Damnatio Memoriae by Michael Meyerhofer

Lotus Buffet by Rupert Fike

The Melancholy MBA by Richard Donnelly

Two-Star General by Grey Held

Chosen by Toni Thomas

Etch and Blur by Jamie Thomas

Water-Rites by Ann E. Michael

Bad Behavior by Michael Steffen

Tracing the Lines by Susanna Lang

Rising to the Rim by Carol Tyx

Treading Water with God by Veronica Badowski

Rich Man's Son by Ron Self

Just Drive by Robert Cooperman

The Alp at the End of My Street by Gary Leising

About the Prize

BRICK ROAD

POETRY PRESS

The Brick Road Poetry Prize, established in 2010, is awarded annually for the best book-length poetry manuscript. Entries are accepted August 1st through November 1st. The winner receives $1000 and publication. For details on our preferences and the complete submission guidelines, please visit our website at www.brickroadpoetrypress.com.

Winners of the Brick Road Poetry Prize

2019
Return of the Naked Man by Robert Tremmel

2018
Speaking Parts by Beth Ruscio

2017
Touring the Shadow Factory by Gary Stein

2016
Assisted Living by Erin Murphy

2015
Lauren Bacall Shares a Limousine by Susan J. Erickson

2014
Battle Sleep by Shannon Tate Jonas

2013
Household Inventory by Connie Jordan Green

2012
The Alp at the End of My Street by Gary Leising

2011
Bad Behavior by Michael Steffen

2010
Damnatio Memoriae by Michael Meyerhofer

www.ingramcontent.com/pod-product-compliance
Lightning Source LLC
Chambersburg PA
CBHW031142090426
42738CB00008B/1183